The Petrisin Guide
To Taking
CLEP Exams

Laura Petrisin

Cover design by Laura Petrisin

Press On
P.O. Box 771
Trumansburg, NY 14886
lpetrisin@peoplepc.com
www.presson-products.com

Foreword

The CLEP examination is one of the best kept secrets of higher education. I first found out about CLEP exams when my daughter, Grace, was going into her high school, senior year. I wish I had known about them sooner. She could have started preparing for CLEP exams in her junior year and I would have purchased her home school materials much differently.

As it was, Grace took and passed two CLEP exams in her senior year and earned six college credits. These credits were later granted by her college of choice, SUNY Binghamton. By taking the CLEP exams, Grace saved a lot of time, and her father and I saved a lot of money. We could have saved even more if we had found out about the advantages of CLEP sooner. The purpose of this guide is to present the facts about earning college credit through CLEP exams as simply and painlessly as possible, and to share its benefits with other educators.

- Laura Petrisin

Table of Contents

Introduction

The what, why, where, when, and how of CLEP:

What is CLEP? CLEP stands for College - Level Examination Program. It is a means of earning college credit without the classes, and at a much lower cost than tuition. CLEP is a series of exams in over 30 college level courses developed by the College Board. This is the same group that developed the SAT and AP exams. Each exam passed is credit earned toward a college degree. CLEP exams cover the introductory or lower level course material that students are often required to take during their first two years of college. CLEP fulfills general education requirements. There are 2,900 colleges and universities that accept CLEP credit. That number represents most institutions, but not all. The chances are good however, that your school of choice will be among those that do grant credit.

Why take a CLEP exam? There are numerous reasons and they are all advantageous to everybody, but especially to the homeschooled student. Here's why:

• **#1 Save money!** You can save thousands of dollars in college tuition cost. The cost of a CLEP exam is $77.00, a fraction of tuition costs for the same course. Used college textbooks can often be bought online for less than half the price of a new book.

• **#2 Save time!** You can save hundreds of hours of classroom time by taking CLEP exams. A passed CLEP exam can earn you from 3 to 12 credits depending on your college's CLEP policy.

• **#3 Fulfill high school requirements while earning college credit at the same time with the same course material.** Kill two birds with one stone! For the homeschooler, that is a wise investment!

• **#4 Figure out what you want to do in life.** Take advantage of the opportunity to explore different subject matter in order to narrow your career interests and choose your field of study.

• **#5 Gain knowledge and confidence!** Successfully passing the college level exams can alleviate possible apprehensions in regard to the difficulty of college course work.

1.

• **#6 Flexibility of study time and when to schedule the exam.** You decide when you want to register for the CLEP exam and how much study time you need to prepare for it.

Where can I take a CLEP exam? There are over 1,600 CLEP testing centers worldwide. Most centers are at colleges and universities in the U.S.

When can I take a CLEP exam? CLEP exams are administered at testing centers throughout the year. Once you have located a convenient center, you can contact that center directly for information about registration, scheduling, and fees.

How do I take a CLEP exam? This guide will help you through the process of choosing, registering, preparing for, and taking CLEP exams. If you have decent study habits, you should be able to pass a CLEP exam without difficulty. So, let's get started!

Getting Started

Four Steps To Getting Started With CLEP:

Step #1 - Decide which CLEP exams to take.
Step #2 - Find out the CLEP policy of your prospective college.
Step #3 - Find a test center and register to take your exams.
Step #4 - Choose the right study materials.

Step #1 Decide which exams to take.

There are 33 CLEP exams. Each exam is 90 minutes long and is primarily made up of multiple choice questions with the exception of the College Composition exam. A few exams also contain fill-ins. Below is a basic list of the exams under their general areas of study. The next chapter gives descriptions of the exams.

Composition and Literature - 6 Exams
American Literature, Analyzing and Interpreting Literature, College Composition, College Composition Modular, English Literature, and Humanities.

Foreign Languages - 3 Exams
French Language (Levels 1 and 2), German Language (Levels 1 and 2), and Spanish Language (Levels 1 and 2)

History and Social Sciences - 12 Exams
American Government, Human Growth and Development, Introduction to Educational Psychology, Introductory Psychology, Introductory Sociology, Principles of Macroeconomics, Principles of Microeconomics, Social Sciences and History, History of the United States I: Early Colonization to 1877, History of the United States II: 1865 to the Present, Western Civilization I: Ancient Near East to 1648, and Western Civilization II: 1648 to the Present.

Science and Mathematics - 7 Exams
Biology, Calculus, Chemistry, College Algebra, College Mathematics, Natural Sciences, and Precalculus.

Business - 5 Exams

Financial Accounting, Introductory Business Law, Information Systems and Computer Applications, Principles of Management, and Principles of Marketing.

Step #2 - Find out your college's CLEP policy.

Go to www.collegeboard.com/student/testing/clep/about.html. On the left hand side of the page, there will be links. Under the heading of Tools, you will find the "Colleges Granting CLEP Credit" link. Click that and you will be taken to a page where you can search for CLEP colleges by state and city or name. There is also a search box for international CLEP colleges for those interested.

If your school is listed, the address and phone number will also be listed with it. Check directly with the institution to make sure that it grants credit for CLEP, and review the specifics of its policy.

A college will typically list its academic policies in its general catalogue. The CLEP policy can usually be found under a heading such as Credit-by-Examination, Advanced Standing, Advanced Placement, or External Degree Program. It's also pretty easy to find out a college's CLEP policy by way of its website. Most college websites have search boxes. Type in "CLEP" and you can get your information pretty quickly. Another way to find out what you need to know is by calling the college's admissions and inquiring there. Here are the things you want to find out:

- How much CLEP credit can you earn? Many CLEP exams are designed to correspond to one-semester courses. Some even correspond to full-year or two-year courses. As stated, many colleges grant course credit for CLEP exams. However, not all colleges may award the same amount of CLEP credit. Each college sets its own policy regarding the CLEP exams it will accept and how many credits it will award. You may want to research colleges that grant credit for all or most of the CLEP exams.

- What is the college's required score for passing the exam and earning CLEP credit? The College Board's recommended credit granting score is a 50 (on a 20-80 scale). A college may go with the College Board's recommended score of 50 or it may decide its own required score which could vary from exam to exam. Find out the college's minimum qualifying score for each exam you're considering.

4.

Step # 3 - Find a CLEP test center and register to take your exams.

CLEP exams are administered at approximately 1,600 test centers on college campuses in the U.S. and around the world. To find a test center near you, go to http://www.collegeboard.com/clep. On the menu to the left, you will see the "CLEP Test Centers" link underneath the Tools heading. Click on that link and you will be taken to a page where you can search for CLEP test centers by state and city or by typing in your zip code and finding centers within 50 miles distance from your home. You can also search for test centers by college name, and international test centers by country. CLEP test centers will have their addresses and phone numbers listed, so that you can contact them directly. You must contact your test center to find out its registration procedures, scheduled test dates, and payment policies.

* Note: You may not repeat a CLEP exam of the same title within six months. Scores of exams repeated earlier than six months will be canceled and test fees forfeited.

- Complete a Registration Form and mail it with payment to your test center. A CLEP Registration Form (.pdf/336k) can be downloaded from http://www. collegeboard.com/student/testing/clep/reg.html. Some institutions use their own forms or have online registration procedures. Others require that registration information be given at the testing center on the day of the exam. Find out the registration procedure of your testing center by calling them!

- Test fees must be paid by credit card (preferred method of payment) or check or money order made payable to "College-Level Examination Program." Each exam is $77.00. Most test centers charge an administration fee directly payable to the institution. Contact the test center directly to find out the exact amount of the fee. Each test center has its own policy and may charge a different amount.

*Tip: Remember the exam fee ($77) is payable to the "College-Level Examination Program. The test administration fee is payable to the institution where the test is administered.

Step # 4 - Choose Study Materials.

After deciding which exam to take, the next step is to choose the corresponding study materials. The Official CLEP Study Guide can be obtained through the College Board website. The guide gives you an idea of the topics that will be covered in all exams. It also gives a broad sample of the type of questions that will be asked. It's a good investment, especially if you're planning to take more than two CLEP exams. The CLEP Study Guide by itself, however, does not have sufficient information to pass the exam. A college textbook is also recommended. Search a college website or call the college for a syllabus of a course equivalent to the CLEP exam you plan to take. Find out what textbook or reading material is required for that course. Then, check the content page of the textbook to make sure the topics listed there match the content and description of the CLEP exam you've chosen. You can also download the CLEP sampler from the College Board website which shows the format of questions on the test.

There are many online resources to take advantage of as well. In the next chapter you will find recommended study resources at the end of each exam description.

CLEP* Exam Descriptions

CLEP exams are administered via computer and are available year-round. All exams are scored on a scale of 20 to 80, and the recommended minimum-credit-granting score for all exams is 50, a score representative of a grade of C. Score reports are available immediately upon completion of the exam with the exception of the College Composition which includes a mandatory essay. Those results are mailed out after the essay section has been scored.

The following exam descriptions give a general idea of each exam's content. Study resources are also included. The resources are mostly comprised of college texts and study guides. I recommend getting the CLEP Official Study Guide because it gives you a good idea of what you're going to be tested on for each exam. You can use this information to help select your college text and any other resources.

I. Composition and Literature - 6 Exams

Most of the Composition and Literature tests are about 90 minutes long except for the College Composition which is two hours long. Exams are composed primarily of multiple-choice questions, although some exams include a small number of fill-in or ordering questions. The College Composition exam is the only exam that includes a mandatory essay. There is no additional fee for this essay. Other Composition and Literature exams may have optional ssays. Some colleges require these essays and some do not. The essays are graded by the faculty at the institution requiring them. There is a small, additional fee for taking an optional essay, payable to the institution that administers the exam.

American Literature - 6 credits

The American Literature exam covers material usually taught in a two-semester introductory or survey college course. It deals with the prose and poetry written in America from Colonial times to the present. The exam tests knowledge of literary works during this period along with the ability to understand and interpret them. The following knowledge and skills are required:

• **45-60%: Knowledge of Literary Works:** The authors, plots,

7.

characters, style, settings, themes of particular literary work.
• **25-40%: Interpreting Literary Works**: Poems or excerpts from long poems and prose.
• **10-15%: Knowledge of the Social and Historical Settings of Specific Works and Authors**: The relationships between literary works and traditions.
• **5-10%: Critical Theories:** Of American writers, literary terms, and verse forms.

The subject matter of the exam covers the following time periods:

- 15% - Colonial and Early National Period (Up to 1830)
- 25% - Romantic Period (1830-1870)
- 20% - Period of Realism and Naturalism (1870-1910)
- 25% - Modernist Period (1910-1945)
- 15% - Contemporary Period (1945-present)

The test contains 100 questions to be answered in 90 minutes. An optional essay section can be taken in addition to the multiple choice test.

Study Resources:
- *American Literature - Barron's E-Z 101 Study Keys* - Covers three centuries of American prose and poetry, including present-day trends and influences. Authors are listed in historical/literary time periods and in chronological order. Each key is an introduction to the author with examples of the author's works.
- Baym, ed, *Norton Anthology of American Literature* (Norton)
- Harmon, William, *A Handbook to Literature* (Prentice Hall)
- *CLEP Official Study Guide* - This is the official, basic guide to all CLEP exams. It contains sample questions and answer keys for each exam.

 * Tip: Save money by purchasing used college textbooks and study guides at websites such as amazon.com, textbooks.com, campusbooks.com and many others. Do a google search!

Analyzing and Interpreting Literature - 6 credits

The Analyzing and Interpreting Literature exam covers material generally taught in a two-semester, undergraduate, literature course. It tests the ability to analyze and interpret literary passages from fiction, non-fiction, poetry, and drama. Examples of some skills required are the abilities to analyze elements such as meaning, tone, imagery, and style. The exam also assesses the ability to interpret metaphors and to recognize rhetorical devices. The literary passages are supplied in the test and previous experience with them is not needed to answer the questions. The passages are primarily taken from American and British literature. The subject matter of the exam covers the following time periods:

- 3 - 7%: Classical and pre-Renaissance
- 20 - 30%: Renaissance and 17th century
- 35 - 45%: 18th and 19th centuries
- 25 - 35%: 20th and 21st centuries

The exam contains approximately 80 multiple choice questions to be answered in 90 minutes. An optional essay can be taken in addition to the multiple choice test.

Study Resources:
- *CLEP Analyzing & Interpreting Literature* (REA) Research and Education Association. Included in this book are three practice exams that provide detailed explanations for all exam questions.
- Roberts, Edgar et al., *Literature: An Introduction to Reading and Writing* (Prentice Hall)
- *CLEP Official Study Guide*

* Tip: Check out the forum at www.degreeforum.net for a look at study and testing strategies. You'll see questions and answers from people who either plan on taking a CLEP exam or have already taken one. Good discussion and helpful advice!

College Composition - 6 credits & College Composition Modular- 3 to 6 credits

The College Composition and College Composition Modular examinations assess writing skills that include analysis, argumentation, synthesis, usage, and research.

- **10%: Conventions of Standard Written English :** Syntax, Sentence boundaries, Recognition of correct sentences, Concord/agreement, Diction, Modifiers, Idiom, Active/passive voice,

Logical comparison, Logical Agreement, and Punctuation.
• **40%: Revision Skills:** Organization, Evaluation of evidence, Awareness of audience, tone, and purpose, Level of detail, Sentence and paragraph coherence, Main idea, thesis, statements, and topic sentences, Rhetoric, Use of language, Evaluation of author's authority and appeal, Consistency of point of view, Transitions, and Sentence-level errors.
• **25%: Ability to Use Source Materials:** Use of reference materials, Evaluation of sources, Integration of resource material, and Documentation of sources.
• **25%: Rhetorical Analysis:** Appeals, Tone, Organization/structure, Rhetorical effects, Use of language, and Evaluation of evidence.

College Composition contains multiple-choice items and two mandatory, centrally scored essays. The two essays measure the candidate's ability to write clearly and effectively. The first essay is based on reading observation or experience. The second essay requires the candidate to synthesize and cite from two sources that are provided. Essays must be typed on the computer. After each College Composition exam is administered, college English faculty from throughout the country score the essays via an online scoring system.

Each of the two essays is scored independently by two different readers, and the scores are then combined. This combined score is weighted with the score from the multiple-choice section. These scores are then combined to yield the candidate's total score.

College Composition contains approximately 50 multiple-choice items to be answered in 50 minutes and two essays to be written in 70 minutes.

College Composition Modular does not include a mandatory essay. However, colleges may elect to supplement the modular version of the exam with an essay available from CLEP or with a writing assessment of their own. The exam contains all multiple-choice questions, and is supplemented either with an essay section provided by the college, or one provided by CLEP and scored by the college. College Composition Modular is available for colleges that want a valid, reliable multiple-choice assessment and greater local control over the direct writing assessment. The percentages of exam questions on each topic are the same in both exams.

College Composition Modular contains approximately 90 questions to be answered in 90 minutes and, depending on the option chosen, two essays to be written in 70 minutes.

The American Council on Education (ACE) has recommended the awarding of **six credit hours** for a score of 50 on the CLEP College Composition exam.

ACE recommends the awarding of **three credit** hours for a score of 50 on the 90 minute, multiple choice College Composition Modular exam. If colleges choose to supplement the modular version of the exam with an essay, the credit recommendation is **six credit hours**.

Study Resources:
- Bishop and Strickland, *The Subject Is Writing: Essays by Teachers and Students,* (Boynton/Cook)
- Bullock, *The Norton Field Guide to Writing,* (W.W. Norton)
- *CLEP Official Study Guide*

Online Resources:
- DePaul Universtiy School for New Learning: Writing Guide - Very good resource of clear basic guidelines to the writing process.

English Literature - 6 credits

The English Literature exam covers the prose, poetry, and drama written by British and other authors from Beowulf to the present. It requires familiarity with major authors, literary works, literary terms (ie. metaphor and personification), and basic literary forms (ie. sonnet and ballad). It measures both knowledge and ability in the following:

   • **35 - 40%: Knowledge of Literary Background:** Identification of authors, metrical patterns, and literary terms and references.
   • **60 - 65%: Ability to Analyze Elements In a Literary Passage:** Perceive meanings, identify tone and mood, follow imagery, identify style and comprehend the reasoning of literary criticism.

The exam contains approximately 95 question to be answered in 90 minutes. An optional essay is also available. The essay is only required if the college, to which you are applying, requests a writing sample. Three essay topics are presented and you must respond to two. An essay on the first topic, a persuasive analysis of a poem, is required. The recommended time to spend on this is 35-40 minutes. For the second essay, you must choose one of two topics that present a specific theme, position or observation. You then choose any work by a particular author to support the claim of your chosen topic. Or, if you prefer, you can select works from a list that is provided.

Study Resources:
- Abrams, M. H.; Greenblatt, Stephen, *The Norton Anthology of English Literature* (Norton)
- *Longman Anthology of British Literature*, (Longman)
- *CLEP Official Study Guide*

*Tip: Find sample questions for the CLEP English Literature exam at www.clepexampracticetests.com/english-lit.html.

Humanities - 6 credits

The Humanities exam tests general knowledge of literature, art, music, and other performing arts. Its coverage is broad with questions on poetry, prose, philosophy, art, architecture, music, dance, theater, and film. Time periods from classical to contemporary are presented. It requires an understanding of the humanities through recollection of specific information, comprehension and application of concepts, and analysis and interpretation of a variety of artistic works. The following knowledge and skills are required:

- **50%: Knowledge of factual information :** Such as authors, works, etc.
- **30%: Recognition of techniques:** Such as rhyme scheme, medium, and style.
- **20%: Interpretation:** Of literary passages and art reproductions.

The exam contains 140 questions to be answered in 90 minutes. The subject matter consists of 50% Literature and 50% of the Arts.

Study Reources:
- Adams, *Exploring the Humanities* (Prentis Hall).
- Martin, *Humanities Through the Arts* (McGraw-Hill)
- *CLEP Official Study Guide*

II. Foreign Languages - 3 Exams

Most colleges that award credit for a Foreign Language exam, award either two or four semesters of credit depending on test scores.

French Language - Up to 12 credits

The French Language exam measures the knowledge and ability equivalent to that of two to four semesters of college French language study. The ability to understand spoken and written French must be demonstrated. The exam contains 120 questions to be answered in 90 minutes. There are three sections:

- **15%: Section I - Listening:** Rejoinders - Choosing the best responses to short spoken prompts.
- **25%: Section II - Listening:** Dialogues and Narratives - Choosing answers to questions based on longer spoken selections.
- **60%: Section III - Reading:** Discrete sentences, short cloze passages, and reading comprehension.

Study Resources:
- Bragger and Ruce, *Allons-y!: Le Français par é tapes* (Heinle)
- Crocker, *Shaum's Outline of French Grammar* (McGraw-Hill)
- Jansma and Kassen, *Motifs!* (Thompson and Heinle)
- Muyskens et al., *Bravo!* (Heinle)

Online Resources:
- Bonjour de France!
- Carnegie Mellon University: Open Learning Initiative - French 1&2
- Manchester Metropolitan Universtiy: Real French.net

German Language - Up to 12 credits

The German Language exam measures the knowledge and ability equivalent to that of two to four semesters of college German language study. The exam contains approximately 120 questions to be answered in 90 minutes. There are three sections:

- **15%: Section I - Listening:** Rejoinders - Understanding the spoken language through everyday situations.

• **25%: Section II - Listening:** Dialogue and Narratives - Understanding the spoken language in longer dialogues and narratives.
• **60%: Section III - Reading:** Discrete sentences, short cloze passages, and reading comprehension.

Study Resources:
- DiDonato et al., *Deutsch: Na Klav!* (McGraw-Hill)
- Jannach and Korb, *German for Reading Knowledge* (Heinle)
- Treffpunkt, *Deutsch* (Prentice Hall)

Online Resources:
- E.L. Easton Languages Online: German
- Goethe - Institut: Learning German
- Young Germany

Spanish Language - Up to 12 credits

The Spanish Language exam measures the knowledge and ability equivalent to two to four semesters of college Spanish language study. The exam contains 120 questions to be answered in 90 minutes. There are three sections:

• **15%: Section I - Listening**: Rejoinders - Listening comprehension through short oral exchanges.
• **25%: Section II - Listening:** Dialogue and Narratives - Listening comprehension through longer spoken selections.
• **60%: Section III - Reading:** Discrete sentences, short cloze passages, and reading comprehension.

Study Resources:
- Iglesias and Meiden, *Spanish for Oral and Written Review* (Heinle)
- Gilman et al., *Nuevos Horizontes* (Wiley)
- Valdes and Teschner, *Español Escrito (*Prentice Hall)

Online Resources:
- StudySpanish.com
- Trent Universtiy: Spanish Language Exercises

III. History and Social Sciences - 12 Exams

American Government - 3 credits

The American Government exam covers material taught in a one-semester introductory college course in American government and politics. It covers federal institutions and policy processes, federal courts and civil liberties, political parties and interest groups, political beliefs and behavior, and the content and history of the Constitution.

The exam contains approximately 100 questions to be answered in 90 minutes.

Study Resources:
- Bardes et al., *American Government and Politics Today: The Essentials* (Wadsworth)
- O'Brien et al., *Government by the People* (Prentice Hall)
- Wilson, *American Government* (Wadsworth)
- *CLEP Official Study Guide*

Online Resources:
- Hippocampus: American Government
- Citizen Joe
- National Repository of Online Courses: American Government

* Tip: Go to www.4tests.com/exams to try your hand at sample CLEP exam questions in the following subjects: English, Humanities, Psychology, Math, Sciences, Macro Economics, Management, Marketing, Micro Economics, Social Science, and American Government.

History of the United States I: Early Colonization to 1877 - 3 credits

The History of the United States I exam covers material taught in the first semester of a two-semester college course in U.S. history. It covers the time period from early European colonization to the end of Reconstruction (1790-1877). Themes include colonial life, black slavery, abolitionism, and reform movements, immigration, Native American culture, major movements in the history of women and the family, the changing role of religion, the Constitution and its amendments, the development and expansion of democracy, the changing role of government, political parties, nationalism, major movements in the history of American literature, art, and culture, economic growth and development, and the causes and impacts of major wars in U.S. history.

The exam contains approximately 120 questions to be answered in 90 minutes.

Study Resources:
- Boyer et al., *The Enduring Vision* (Wadsworth)
- Garraty, John, *The American Nation, A History of the United States to 1877*
- Goldfield et al., *American Journey* (Prentice Hall)
- *CLEP Official Study Guide*

Online Resources:
- Hippocampus: US History
- National Repository of Online Courses: U.S. History I & U.S. History II

The History of the United States II:
1865 to the Present - 3 credits

The History of the United States II exam covers material taught in the second semester of a two-semester college course in U.S. history. It covers the time period from the end of the Civil War to the present with most of the questions focusing on the twentieth century.

Among the topics tested are American expansionism, Constitutional amendments and their interpretations by the Supreme Court, agricultural life, political parties, political expressions of liberalism, conservatism and other movements, regulatory and welfare legislation, demographic trends, economic growth and development, labor organization, immigration, urbanization and industrialization, major movements in the history of American arts, trends in the history of women and the family, and the causes and impacts of major wars in American history.

The examination contains 120 questions to be answered in 90 minutes.

Study Resources:
- Brinkley, Alan, *American History: A Survey, Volume 2, Since 1865* (Mc-Graw-Hill)
- Nash et al., *The American People: Creating a Nation and a Society,* Concise Edition, Volume 2 (since 1865), (Prentice Hall)
- *CLEP Official Study Guide*

Online Resources:
- Hippocampus: US History
- National Repository of Online Courses: U.S. History I & U.S. History II

Human Growth and Development - 3 credits

The Human Growth and Development exam covers material taught in a one-semester introductory college course in psychology or human development through infancy, childhood, adolescence, adulthood, and aging.

Knowledge and skills are tested in the following: Theoretical perspectives, research strategies and methods, biological development throughout the life span, perceptual development throughout the life span, cognitive development throughout the life span, language development, intelligence throughout the life span, social development throughout the life span, family, home, and society throughout the life span, personality and emotion, learning, schooling, work and interventions, and atypical development.

The exam contains approximately 90 questions to be answered in 90 minutes.

Study Resources:
- Berger, Kathleen, *The Developing Person Through the Life Span, 6th Ed.,* (Worth)
- Berryman et al., *Developmental Psychology and You* (Wiley)
- Boyd and Bee, *Lifespan Development (*Allyn & Bacon)
- Craig and Dunn, *Understanding Human Development* (Prentice Hall)
- *CLEP Official Study Guide*

Online Resources:
- Tufts OpenCourseWare: PPM 100 Human Growth and Development

Introduction to Educational Psychology - 3 credits

The Introduction to Educational Psychology exam covers material taught in a one-semester introductory college course. It places emphasis on principles of learning and cognition, teaching methods and classroom management, child growth and development, and evaluation and assessment of learning. The exam tests the following topics:

- **5%: Educational Aims and Philosophies:** Lifelong learning, moral/character development, preparation for careers, preparation for responsible citizenship, and socialization.
- **15%: Cognitive Perceptive:** Attention and perception, chunking/encoding, memory capacity, mental imagery, long-term memory, problem solving and transfer.
- **11%: Behavioristic Perspective:** Applications of behaviorism, behavioral modification, classical conditioning, cognitive learning theory, law of effect, operant conditioning, reinforcement, and token economies.
- **15%: Development:** Adolescence, cognitive, gender identity and sex roles, language acquisition, mental health, moral, social, school readiness.
- **10%: Motivation:** Achievement, anxiety/stress, locus of control, learned helplessness, intrinsic motivation, reinforcement contingencies, and theories of motivation.
- **17%: Individual Differences:** Aptitude/achievement, creativity, cultural influences, exceptionalities in learning, intelligence, nature vs. nurture, and reading ability.
- **12%: Testing:** Assessment of Objectives, bias in testing, class room assessment, descriptive statistics, norm- and criterion- referenced tests, scaled scores/standard deviation, test construction, and assessment techniques.
- **10%: Pedagogy:** Advance organizers, classroom management, cooperative learning, discovery and reception learning, instructional design and technique, psychology of content areas, and teacher expectations/Pygmalion effect/wait time.

The exam contains approximately 100 questions to be answered in 90 minutes.

Study Resources:
- Ormrod, *Educational Psychology: Developing Learners* (Prentice Hall)
18.

- Santrock, *Educational Psychology* (McGraw-Hill)
- Slavin, *Educational Psychology: Theory Into Practice* (Allyn & Bacon)
- *CLEP Official Study Guide*

Online Resources:
- Valdosta State University: Educational Psychology Interactive

Principles of Macroeconomics - 3 credits

The Principles of Macroeconomics exam covers material taught in a one-semester undergraduate course. It deals with principles of economics that apply to an economy as a whole, particularly the general price level, output and income, and interrelations among economy sectors. Particular emphasis is placed on aggregate demand and supply, and on monetary and fiscal policy tools used to achieve policy objectives. Understanding is required in concepts such as gross domestic product, consumption, investment, unemployment, inflation, inflationary gap, and recessionary gap. Knowledge is assessed in the following topics: The Federal Reserve Bank, income, employment price level, deficits, and interest rate. There should also be a basic understanding of foreign exchange markets, balance of payments, effects of currency, and appreciation/depreciation of a country's imports and exports.

- **8 - 12%: Basic Economic Concepts:** Scarcity, choice, and opportunity costs, production possibilities curve, comparative advantage, specialization, and exchange, demand, supply, and market balance, and macroeconomic issues.
- **12 - 16%: Measurement of Economic Performance:** National income accounts, inflation measurement and adjustment, and unemployment.
- **10 - 15%: National Income and Price Determination:** Aggregate demand and supply, and macroeconomic equilibrium.
- **15 - 20%: Financial Sector:** Money, banking and financial assets, Central bank and control of the money supply.
- **20 - 30%: Inflation, Unemployment, and Stabilization Policies.**
- **5 - 10%: Economic Growth and Productivity:** Investment in human and physical capital, research, development, and technological progress, and growth policy.
- **10 - 15%: International Trade and Finance:** Balance of payment accounts, foreign exchange market, export and capital flows, and links to financial and good markets.

The exam contains approximately 80 questions to be answered in 90 minutes.

Study Resources:
- Colander, *Macroeconomics and Microeconomics* (McGraw-Hill)
- Gottheil, *Principles of Macroeconomics* (Thomson/Cengage)
- Krugman and Wells, *Macroeconomics and Microeconomics* (Worth)
- *CLEP Official Study Guide*

Online Resources:
- Carnegie Mellon University: Open Learning Initiative - Introductory Economics
- University of California, Berkeley: Webcast lecture for Economics 100B

Principles of Microeconomics - 3 credits

The Principles of Microeconomics exam is taught in a one-semester introductory college course. It deals with the analysis of both consumer and business behavior in the economy. There should be an understanding of how the free markets work, how consumers make decisions to maximize utility, and how individual firms make decisions to maximize profits. The exam requires the abilities to identify market structures and to analyze the behavior of firms in terms of price and output decisions. There should also be the ability to evaluate market outcome, to identify cases in which private markets fail to allocate resources efficiently, and to explain how government intervention fixes or fails to fix the resource allocation problem. It is also important to understand the determination of wages and to evaluate the distribution of income. Knowledge and skills are required in the following:

- **8 - 14%: Basic Economic Concepts:** Scarcity, choice, specialization, trade, economic systems, property rights and the role of incentives, and marginal analysis.
- **55 - 70%: The Nature and Functions of Product Markets:** Supply and demand, theory of consumer choice, production and costs, firm behavior and market structure.
- **10 - 18%: Factor Markets:** Derived factor demand, marginal revenue product, labor market and market distribution of income.
- **12 - 18%: Market Failure and the Role of Government:** Externalities, public goods, public policy to promote competition, and income distribution.

The exam contains approximately 80 questions to be answered in 90 minutes.

Study Resources:
- Baumol and Blinder, *Microeconomics: Principles & Policy* (South-Western)
- Mankiw, *Brief Principles of Macroeconomics and Brief Principles of Microeconomics* (South-Western)
- Salvatore, *Schaum's Outline of Microeconomics* (McGraw-Hill)
- *CLEP Official Study Guide*

Online Resources:
- Carnegie Mellon University: Open Learning Initiative - Introductory Economics
- Economics Department at SUNY Oswego: Online Economics Textbooks

Introductory Psychology - 3 credits

The Introductory Psychology exam covers material that is taught in a one-semester undergraduate course. It requires knowledge of terminology, principles, and theory. There should also be the ability to comprehend, evaluate, and analyze problem situations along with the ability to apply knowledge to new situations.

- **8 - 9%: History, Approaches, and Methods:** History of psychology, biological, behavioral, cognitive, humanistic, and psychodynamic approaches, research methods and ethics in research.
- **8 - 9%: Biological Bases of Behavior:** Endocrine system, etiology, functional organization of the nervous system, geneics, neuroanatomy, and physiological techniques.
- **7 - 8%: Sensation and Perception:** Attention, other senses, perceptional development and processes, receptor processes and sensory mechanisms.
- **5 - 6%: States of Consciousness:** Hypnosis and meditation, psycho-active drug effects, sleep and dreaming.
- **10 - 11%: Learning:** Biological bases, classical conditioning, cognitive process in learning, observational learning, and operant conditioning.
- **8 - 9%: Cognition:** Intelligence and creativity, language, memory, thinking and problem solving.
- **7 - 8%: Motivation and Emotion:** Biological bases, hunger,

thirst, sex, pain, social motivation, theories of emotion and theories of motivation.

• **8 - 9%: Developmental Psychology:** Dimensions of development: physical, cognitive, social, and moral, gender identity and sex roles, heredity - environment issues, longitudinal and cross- sectional research methods and theories of development.

• **7 - 8%: Personality:** Assessment techniques, growth and adjustment, personality theories and approaches, idiographic and nomothetic research methods, self-concept and self-esteem.

• **8 - 9%: Psychological Disorders and Health:** Affective, anxiety, dissociative, personality and somatoform disorders, health, stress and coping, psychoses and theories of psychology.

• **7 - 8%: Treatment of Psychological Disorders:** Behavioral, biological, drug, cognitive and insight therapies, community and preventive approaches.

• **7 - 8%: Social Psychology:** Aggression/antisocial behavior, attitudes and attitude change, attribution processes, conformity, compliance and obedience, group dynamics and interpersonal perception.

• **3 - 4%: Statistics, Test, and Measurement:** Descriptive and inferential statistics, measurement of intelligence, mental handicapping condition, reliability and validity, samples, populations and norms, and types of tests.

The exam contains approximately 95 questions to be answered in 90 minutes.

Study Resources:
- Feldman, *Essentials of Understanding Psychology* (McGraw-Hill)
- Rosenberg and Kosslyn, *Psychology in Context* (Allyn & Bacon)
- Zimbardo, et al., *Psychology: Core Concepts* (Allyn & Bacon)
- *CLEP Official Study Guide*

Online Resources:
- Hippocampus: Psychology
- National Repository of Online Courses: Psychology
- Athabasca University: Centre for Psychology Resources

Introductory Sociology - 3 credits

The Introductory Sociology exam covers material presented in a one-semester college course. It emphasizes basic facts and concepts as well as general theoretical approaches used by sociologists. Knowledge and skills are required to identify specific names, facts, and concepts from sociological literature. There should be an understanding of relationships between concepts, empirical generalizations, theoretical propositions of sociology, and methods by which sociological relationships are established. The exam tests the application of concepts, propositions, and methods to hypothetical situations as well as the interpretation of tables and charts.

- **20%: Institutions:** Economic, educational, family, medical, political, and religious.
- **15%: Social Patterns:** Community, demography, human ecology, and rural/urban patterns.
- **20%: Social Processes:** Collective behavior and social movements, culture, groups and organizations, deviance and social control, socialization, social change and interaction.
- **30%: Social Stratification:** Aging, power and social inequality, race and ethnic relations, professions, occupations, social class and mobility.
- **15%: The Sociological Perspective:** History of sociology, methods, and sociological theory.

The examination contains 100 questions to be answered in 90 minutes.

Study Resources:
- Henslin, *Essentials of Sociology* (Allyn & Bacon)
- Macionis, *Society: The Basics* (Prentice Hall)
- Tischler, *Introduction to Sociology* (Wadsworth)
- *CLEP Official Study Guide*

Online Resources:
- Essentials of Sociology, Anthody Giddens: Online Chapter Review
- Trinity University: General Sociological Links

Social Sciences and History - 3 credits

The Social Sciences and History exam is not based on any specific course but rather, it covers a wide range of topics in the social sciences and history disciplines. Its content is drawn from introductory college courses in U.S. history, Western civilization, world history, government/political science, sociology, geography, psychology, economics, and anthropology. The exam requires familiarity with terminology, facts, conventions, methodology, concepts, principles, generalizations, and theories. There should be an ability to interpret and analyze graphic, pictorial, and written material as well as an ability to apply hypotheses, concepts, theories, and principles to given data.

- **40%: History:** U.S. History, Western Civilization, and World History.
- **13%: Government/Political Science:** Comparative politics, international relations, methods, U.S. institutions, voting and political behavior.
- **11%: Geography:** Cartographic methods, cultural, physical, and regional geography, population and spatial interaction.
- **10%: Economics:** Economic measurements, international trade, major theorists and schools, monetary and fiscal policy, product and resource markets, scarcity, choice, and cost.
- **10%: Psychology:** Aggression, biopsychology, conformity, group process, major theorists and schools, methods, performance, personality, and socialization.
- **10%: Sociology:** Demography, deviance, family, interaction, major theorists and schools, methods, social change, organization, stratification, and theory.
- **6%: Anthropology:** Cultural anthropology, ethnography, major theorists and schools, methods, and paleoanthropology.

The exam contains approximately 120 questions to be answered in 90 minutes.

Study Resources:
Study resources for other CLEP exams would prove helpful for the Social Sciences and History exam. Of particular use are materials for the following exams: American Government, History of the U.S. I and II, Principles of Macroeconomics and Principles of Microeconomics, Introductory Psychology, Introductory Sociology, and Western Civilization I and II.

Western Civilization I - 3 credits

The Western Civilization I: Ancient Near East to 1648 exam covers material that is taught in the first semester of a two-semester course. Questions deal with the civilizations of Ancient Greece, Rome, and the Near East; the Middle Ages; the Renaissance and Reformation; and early modern Europe. The exam requires the ability to choose the correct definition of a historical term, match a historical figure with his/her political view point, identify the correct relationship between two historical factors, or detect the incorrect pairing of an individual with a historical event. It also requires the ability to interpret, evaluate, or relate a passage, map, or picture to other information, or to analyze and utilize the data in a table or graph.

- **8 - 10%: Ancient Near East:** Political evaluation, religion, culture, and technical developments in the Fertile Crescent.
- **15 - 17%: Ancient Greece and Hellenistic Civilization:** Political evolution to Periclean Athens, Periclean Athens to the Pelopon-nesian Wars, culture, religion, and thought of Ancient Greece, the culture, religion, political structure, and thought of Hellenistic Greece.
- **15 - 17%: Ancient Rome:** Political revolution of the Republic and Empire, Roman thought and culture, early Christianity, the Germanic invasions, and the late empire.
- **23 - 27%: Medieval History:** Byzantium and Islam, politics and culture through Charlemagne, feudal and manorial institutions, the medieval church, medieval thought and culture, rise of towns, feudal monarchies and the late medieval church.
- **13 - 17%: Renaissance and Reformation:** The Renaissance in and outside of Italy, the New Monarchies, Protestantism and Catholicism reformed.
- **10 - 15%: Early Modern Europe, 1560 - 1648:** Opening of the Atlantic, Commercial Revolution, dynastic and religious conflicts, thought, and culture.

The exam contains approximately 120 questions to be answered in 90 minutes.

Study Resources:
- Goff, *A Survey of Western Civilization, Vol I* (McGraw-Hill)
- King, *Western Civilization: A Social and Cultural History, Vol I* (Prentice Hall)

25.

- Greer and Lewis, *A Brief History of the Western World* (Wadsworth)
- *CLEP Official Study Guide*

    * Tip: Check out this online resource: "The Internet History Sourcebooks Project." It is a website with modern, medieval and ancient primary source documents, maps, secondary sources, bibliographies, images and music. It was first created in 1996, and is used extensively by teachers as an alternative to history textbooks.

Western Civilization II - 3 credits

    The Western Civilization II: 1648 to the Present exam covers material that is taught in the second semester of a two-semester course. Questions cover European history from the mid-seventeenth century through the post-Second World War period including political, economic, and cultural developments such as Scientific Thought, the Enlightenment, the French and Industrial Revolutions, and the First and Second World Wars. The exam requires the ability to choose the correct definition of a historical term, match a historical figure with his/her political viewpoint, identify the correct relationship between two historical factors, or detect the incorrect pairing of an individual with a historical event. It also requires the ability to interpret, evaluate, or relate a passage, map, or picture to other information, or to analyze and utilize the data in a table or graph.

> • **7 - 9%: Absolutism and Constitutionalism, 1648 - 1715**: The Dutch Republic, the English Revolution, France under Louis XIV, formation of Austria and Prussia, and the "westernization" of Russia.
> • **4 - 6%: Competition for Empire and Economic Expansion:** Global economy of the 18th century, Europe after Utrecht, 1713 - 1740 demographic change in the 18th century.
> • **5 - 7%: The Scientific View of the World:** Major figures of the scientific revolution, new knowledge of man and society, and political theory.
> • **7 - 9%: Period of Enlightenment:** Enlightenment thought, Enlightened despotism, and partition of Poland.
> • **10 - 13%: Revolution and Napoleonic Europe**: The Revolution in France, the Revolution and Europe, the French Empire, and the Congress of Vienna..
> • **7 - 9%: The Industrial Revolution:** Agricultural and Industrial revolution, causes of revolution, economic and social

26.

impact on working and middle class, and the British reform movement.

• **6 - 8%: Political and Cultural Developments, 1815 - 1848:** Conservatism, liberalism, nationalism, socialism, and the Revolutions of 1830 and 1848.

• **8 - 10%: Politics and Diplomacy In the Age of Nationalism, 1850 - 1914:** The unification of Italy and Germany, Austria-Hungary, Russia, France, socialism and labor unions, European diplomacy, 1871 - 1900.

• **7 - 9%: Economy, Culture, and Imperialism, 1850 - 1914:** Demography, world economy of the 19th century, technological developments, science, philosophy, and the arts, imperialism in Africa and Asia.

• **10 - 12%: The First World War and the Russian Revolution:** Causes of the First World War, economic and social impact of the war, the peace settlement, the Revolution of 1917 and its effects.

• **7 - 9%: Europe Between the Wars:** The Great Depression, international politics 1919 - 1939, Stalin's five-year plans and purges, Italy and Germany between the wars, interwar cultural developments.

• **8 - 10%: The Second World War and Contemporary Europe:** The causes and course of the Second World War, postwar Europe, science, philosophy, the arts, and religion, social and political developments.

The exam contains approximately 120 questions to be answered in 90 minutes.

Study Resources:
- Goff, *A Survey of Western Civilization, Vol II* (McGraw-Hill)
- Kishlansky et al., *Civilization in the West* (Pearson Longman)

Online Resource:
- Free University Project: Western Civilization II - 1648 to the Present.

*Remember: When selecting a college textbook, check its table of contents to make sure it matches the knowledge and skills required for the exam you've chosen!

IV. Science and Mathematics

Biology

The Biology exam covers material that is taught in a one-year college general biology course. It tests a knowledge of facts, principles, and processes of biology. The exam also requires an understanding of how information is collected and interpreted, how one hypothesizes from information, and how one draws conclusions and makes predictions. There should be an understanding that science has social consequences. The exam is drawn from the following topics:

- **33%: Molecular and Cellular Biology:** Chemical composition of organisms, cells, enzymes, energy transformations, cell division, and the chemical nature of the gene.
- **34%: Organismal Biology:** Structure and function in plants with emphasis on angiosperms, plant reproduction and development, structure and functions in animals with emphasis on vertebrates, animal reproduction and development, and principles of heredity.
- **33%: Population Biology:** Principles of ecology, principles of evolution, principles of behavior, and social biology.

This exam contains approximately 115 questions to be answered in 90 minutes.

Study Resources:
- Campbell and Reece, *Biology* (Benjamin Cummings)
- Mader, *Essentials of Biology* (McGraw-Hill)
- Raven et al., *Biology* (McGraw-Hill)
- *CLEP Official Study Guide*

Online Resources:
- Hippocampus: Biology
- University of Arizona: The Biology Project
- University of California, Berkeley: Webcast lectures for Biology 1A and 1B
- Online Biology Book: www.emc.maricopa.edu/faculty/farabee/BIOBK/ BioBookTOC.html

*Tip: Check out www.cafegenius.com - Homeschool resources in Math, Science and Languages!

Chemistry

The Chemistry exam covers material taught in a one-year college course. It requires an understanding of the structure and states of matter, reaction types, equations and stoichiometry, equilibrium, kinetics, thermodynamics, and descriptive and experimental chemistry. It also requires the ability to interpret and apply this material to new and unfamiliar problems. During the exam, an online scientific calculator function and a periodic table are available. The subject matter of the exam is drawn from the following topics:

- **20%: Structure of Matter:** Atomic theory and atomic structure, chemical bonding, and nuclear chemistry.
- **19%: States of Matter:** Gases, liquids and solids, and solution
- **12%: Reaction Types:** Formation and cleavage of covalent bonds, precipitation reactions, and oxidation-reduction reactions.
- **10%: Equations and Stoichiometry:** Ionic and molecular species present in chemical systems, stoichiometry: mass and volume relations with emphasis on the mole concept, balancing of equations, including those for redox reactions.
- **7%: Equilibrium:** Concept of dynamic equilibrium, physical and chemical; Le Chatelier's principle; equilibrium constants, and quantitative treatment.
- **4%: Kineti.cs:** Concept of rate of reaction, order of reaction, and rate constant, effect of temperature change on rates, energy of activation and the role of catalysts, and the relationship between the rate-determining step and a mechanism.
- **5%: Thermodynamics:** State Functions:
First Law: Heat of formation and reaction, change in enthalpy, Hess's law, heat capacity, heats of vaporization and fusion.
Second Law: Free energy of formation and reaction, dependence of change in free energy on enthalpy and entropy changes.
Relationship of change in free energy to equilibrium contants and electrode potentials.
- **14%: Descriptive Chemistry:** Chemical reactivity and products

of chemical reactions, relationships in the periodic table, chemistry of the main groups and transition elements, and organic chemistry.
• **9%: Experimental Chemistry:** The basic tools of chemistry and their applications to simple chemical systems: equipment used, observations made, calculations performed, and interpretations of results.

The exam contains approximately 75 questions to be answered in 90 minutes.

Study Resources:
- Goldberg, *Fundamentals of Chemistry* (McGraw-Hill)
- Joesten et al., *The World of Chemistry: Essentials* (Cengage)
- Zumdahl and DeCoste, *Introductory Chemistry* (Cengage)
- *CLEP Official Study Guide*

Online Resources:
- Frostburg State University: General Chemistry Online

Natural Sciences

The Natural Sciences exam covers a wide range of topics taught in introductory courses surveying both biological and physical sciences. The Natural Sciences exam is not intended for those specializing in science. It is meant to test the understanding of basic concepts and principles of science. The exam is drawn from the following topics:

• **50%: Biological Science:** Origin and evolution of life, classification of organisms, cell division and organization, chemical nature of the gene, bioenergetics, biosynthesis, structure, function, and development in organisms, patterns of heredity, concepts of population biology with emphasis on ecology.
• **50%: Physical Science:** Atomic and nuclear structure and properties, elementary particles, nuclear reations, chemical elements, compounds and reactions, molecula structure and bonding, heat, thermodynamics, and states of matter, classical mechanics, relativity, electricity and magnetism, waves, light, and sound, the universe: galaxies, stars, solar system, the earth: atmosphere, hydrosphere, structure features, geologic processes, and history.

The exam contains approximately 120 questions to be answered in 90 minutes.

Study Resources:

To prepare for the Natural Sciences exam, it is advisable to study at least one biological science and one physical science college text book. Check the table of contents against the knowledge and skills required for this test.

Precalculus

The Precalculus exam assesses mastery of skills and concepts required for success in a first-semester calculus course. A large portion of the exam tests the understanding of functions and their properties. Many questions test the knowledge of specific properties of the following types of functions: linear, quadratic, absolute value, square root, polynomial, rational, exponential, logarithmic, trigonometric, inverse trigonometric, and piecewise-defined. Questions present these types of functions symbolically, graphically, verbally, or in tabular form. The Precalculus exam is drawn from the following topics:

- **20%: Algebraic Expressions Equations and Inequalities**
- **15%: Functions:** Concept, properties and operations
- **30%: Representations of Functions:** Symbolic, graphical, and tabular
- **10%: Analytic Geometry**
- **15%: Trigonometry and its Applications**
- **10%: Functions as Models**

The exam contains approximately 48 questions in two sections to be answered in 90 minutes. Section 1 has 25 questions to be answered in 50 minutes. The use of an online graphing calculator (non - CAS) is allowed. Section 2 has 23 questions to be answered in 40 minutes. No calculator is allowed for this section.

*Note: A graphing calculator is available as a free download from collegeboard.com for a 30-day trial period. Students are expected to download the calculator and become familiar with its functionality prior to taking the exam.

Study Resources:
- Axler, *Precalculus: A Prelude to Calculus* (Wiley)
- Huettenmueller, *Pre-Calculus Demystified* (McGraw-Hill)
- Ratti and McWaters, *Precalculus* (Addison-Wesley)
- *CLEP Official Study Guide*

Online Resources:
- Drexel University: Math Tools
- North Carolina State University: Math 107 Lectures
- Temple University: Calculus on the Web—Precalculus Book
- Cafe Genuis: Homeschool Pre-Calculus

   *TIP: Take a practice CLEP Precalculus exam at www.free-test-online.com/clep-math-and-science/clep-precalculus-practice.

Calculus

The Calculus exam covers skills and concepts that are taught in a one-semester college course. The content is comprised of approximately 60% limits and differential calculus and 40% integral calculus. Algebraic, trigonometric, and general functions are included. The exam is primarily concerned with an intuitive understanding of calculus and experience with its methods and applications.

There are two sections of the exam. Section 1 consists of 27 questions to be completed in approximately 50 minutes. A calculator is not permitted during this portion of the exam. Section 2 consists of 17 questions to be completed in approximately 40 minutes. An online graphing calculator is available during this portion of the exam.

*Note: A graphing calculator is available as a free download from collegeboard.com for a 30-day trial period. Students are expected to download the calculator and become familiar with its functionality prior to taking the exam.

The subject matter of the exam is drawn from the following topics:

     • **5%: Limits:** Statement of properties, limits that involve infinity, and continuity.
     • **55%: Differential Calculus:** The derivative and applications of

the derivative.

• **40%: Integral Calculus:** Antiderivatives and techniques of integration, applications of antiderivatives, the definite integral, and applications of the definitive integrals.

Study Resources:
- Bear, *Understanding Calculus* (Wiley-IEEE)
- Neill, *Teach Yourself Calculus* (McGraw-Hill)
- Rogawski, *Calculus* (W. H. Freeman)
- *CLEP Official Study Guide*

Online Resources:
- Drexel University: Math Tools
- Hippocampus: Calculus
- John A. Taylor's Aid for Calculus

*REMEMBER: A graphing calculator is available as a free download from collegeboard.com for a 30-day trial period. Download it and become familiar with its function in preparation for the Calculus exams!

College Algebra

The College Algebra exam covers material that is taught in a one-semester college course. Half of the test is made up of routine problems requiring basic algebraic skills. The remainder involves solving non-routine problems in which an understanding of concepts must be demonstrated. The test places little emphasis on arithmetic calculations and a calculator is not required. The exam is drawn from the following topics:

• **25%: Algebraic Operations:** Factoring and expanding polynomials, operations with algebraic expressions, operations with exponents and properties of logarithms.
• **25%: Equations and Inequalities:** Linear equations and inequalities, quadratic equations and inequalities, absolute value equations and inequalities, systems of equations and inequalities, and exponential and logarithmic equations.
• **30%: Functions and Their Properties:** Definition and interpretation, representation/modeling, domain and range, algebra of

functions, graphs and their properties, and inverse functions.
- **20%: Number Systems and Operations:** Real numbers, complex numbers, sequences and series, factorials and Binomial Theorem, determinants of 2-by-2 matrices.

The exam contains approximately 60 questions to be answered in 90 minutes.

Study Resources:
- Beecher, Penna, and Bittinger, *College Algebra* (Addison-Wesley)
- Huettenmueller, *College Algebra Demystified* (McGraw-Hill)
- Sullivan, *College Algebra Essentials* (Prentice Hall)
- *CLEP Official Study Guide*

Online Resources:
- Armstrong Atlantic State University: College Algebra Tutorial
- Utah State University: Math 1050, College Algebra—Online Independent Study Syllabus
- West Texas A&M University: Virtual Math Lab

 *Tip: Check out www.purplemath.com for some online help and lessons in algebra.**

College Mathematics

The College Mathematics exam covers material taught in a college course for non-mathematics majors. It places little emphasis on arithmetic calculations and does not require the use of a calculator. The exam is drawn from the following topics:

- **10%: Sets:** Union and intersection, subsets, disjoint sets, equivalent sets, Venn diagrams and Cartesian product.
- **10%: Logic:** Truth tables, conjunctions, disjunctions, implications, and negations, conditional statements, necessary and sufficient conditions, converse, inverse, and contrapositive, hypotheses, conclusions, and counter examples.
- **20%: Real Number System:** Prime and composite numbers, odd and even numbers, factors and divisibility, rational and irrational numbers, absolute value and order, open and closed intervals.
- **20%: Functions and Their Graphs:** Properties and graphs of

functions, domain and range, composition of functions and inverse functions, and simple transformations of functions.

• **25%: Probability and Statistics:** Counting problems, computation of probabilities of simple and compound events, simple conditional probability, mean, median, mode, and range, concept of standard deviation, data interpretation: tables, bar, line, and circle graphs, pie charts, scatterplots, and histograms.

• **15%: Additional Topics from Algebra and Geometry:** Complex numbers, logarithms and exponents, applications from algebra and geometry, perimeter and area of plane figures, properties of triangles, circles, and rectangles, the Pythagorean theorem, parallel and perpendicular lines, algebraic equations, systems of linear equations and inequalities, Fundamental Theorem of Algebra, Remainder Theorem and Factor Theorem.

The exam contains approximately 60 questions to be answered in 90 minutes.

Study Resources:
- *CLEP Official Study Guide*
- O'Donell, *Review for the CLEP General Mathematics* (Comex)

Online Resources:
- www.clepinfo.com

*Tip: Check out www.clepinfo.com/study-spot/college-Mathematics.html to get a free study guide and great tips for the College Mathematics exam.

V. Business

Financial Accounting

The Financial Accounting exam covers skills and concepts taught in a first-semester undergraduate course. The exam is drawn from the following topics:

- **20 - 30%: General Topics:** General accounting principles, rules of double-entry accounting, transaction analysis, accounting equation, the accounting cycle, business ethics, purpose of, presentation of, and relationships between financial statements, and forms of business.
- **20 - 30%: The Income Statement:** Presentation format issues, recognition of revenue and expenses, cost of goods sold, irregular items and profitability analysis.
- **30 - 40%: The Balance Sheet:** Cash and internal controls, valuation of accounts, notes receivable, and inventories, acquisition and disposal of long-term asset, depreciation/amortization/depletion, intangible assets, accounts and notes payable, long-term liabilities, owner's equity, preferred and common stock, retained earnings, liquidity, solvency, and activity analysis.
- **5 - 10%: Statement of Cash Flows:** In direct method, cash flow analysis, operating, financing, and investing policies.
- **Less than 5%: Miscellaneous:** Investments, and contingent liabilities

The exam contains approximately 75 questions to be answered in 90 minutes.

Study Resources:
- Horngren et al., *Introduction to Financial Accounting* (Prentice Hall)
- Libby, Libby, and Short, *Financial Accounting* (McGraw-Hill)
- Reimers, *Financial Accounting* (Prentice Hall)
- *CLEP Official Study Guide*

Online Resources:
- MIT OpenCourseWare: Financial Accounting
- Principles of Accounting: Online Textbook

Information Systems and Computer Applications

The Information Systems and Computer Applications exam covers material that is taught in an introductory college course. Questions are equally divided between those testing knowledge, terminology, and basic concepts and those testing the ability to apply that knowledge. The exam is drawn from the following topics:

- **20%: Computer/Telecommunications Hardware and Hardware Functions:** Devices for processing, storage, data entry, telecommunications, network and output, functions performed by computer, telecommunications, and network hardware, digital representation of data for storage and processing, concepts of local-and-wide area network architectures, and concept of mainframe vs. client/server architectures.
- **15%: Computer Software/Programming:** Operating systems and network management systems, software development methods and tools, programming languages, user interfaces, and software packages
- **10%: Data Management:** Data concepts and structures database management systems, hypertext, hypermedia, and SQL, and document images.
- **20%: Information Processing Management:** System develop ment processes and tools, types of information processing applications, system, application, and personal computer security and controls, information processing careers and standards.
- **30%: Information Technology Applications in Organizations:** Analysis, decision support, and expert systems, user applications, office systems, internet and other online services and methods.
- **5%: Social/Ethical Implications and Issues:** Economic effects, privacy concerns, intellectual property rights and legal issues, and effects of information technology on jobs.

The exam contains approximately 100 questions to be answered in 90 minutes.

Study Resources:
- *CLEP Information Systems & Computer Applications* (Ace The CLEP)
- *CLEP Official Study Guide*

💡 ***Tip:** To download a free, sample, practice test for the Information Systems and Computer Applications exam, go to www.petersons. com/pdf/clep_informationsystems_q_print.pdf.

Introductory Business Law

The Introductory Business Law exam covers material that is taught in an introductory one-semester course. The exam places major emphasis on understanding the functions of contracts in American business law and includes questions on the history and sources of American law, legal systems and procedures, agency and employment, and sales. The exam is drawn from the following topics:

- **5 - 10%: History and Sources of American Law/Constitutional Law**
- **5 - 10%: American Legal Systems and Procedures**
- **25 - 35%: Contracts:** Meaning of terms, formation of contracts, capacity, considerations, joint obligations, contracts for the benefit of third parties, assignment/delegation, statute of frauds, scopes and meanings of contracts, breach of contract and remedies, bar to remedies for breach of contract, discharge of contracts, and illegal contracts.
- **25 - 30%: Legal Environment:** Ethics, social responsibility of corporations, government regulations/administrative agencies, environmental law, creditors' rights, product liability, consumer protection, and international business law.
- **10 - 15%: Torts**
- **5 - 10%: Miscellaneous:** Agency, partnerships and corporations, and sales.

The exam contains approximately 100 questions to be answered in 90 minutes.

Study Resources:
- Clarkson, *West's Business Law* (South-Western)
- Emerson, *Business Law* (Barron's)
- Miller, *Business Law Today: The Essentials* (West)
- *CLEP Official Study Guide*

Principles of Management

The Principles of Management exam covers material taught in an introductory course in the essentials of management and organization. It requires a knowledge of human resources and operational and functional aspects of management. The exam is draw from the following topics:

- **15 - 25%: Organization and Human Resources:** Personnel administration, human relations and motivation, training and development, performance appraisal, organizational development, legal concerns, workforce diversity, recruiting and selecting, compensation and benefits, and collective bargaining.
- **10 - 20%: Operational Aspects of Management:** Operations planning and control, work scheduling, total quality management, information processing and management, strategic planning and analysis, and productivity.
- **45 - 55%: Functional Aspects of Management:** Planning, organizing, leading, controlling, authority, decision making, orga-nization charts, organizational structure, budgeting, problem solving, group dynamics and team functions, conflict resolution, communication, change, organizational theory, and historcal aspects.
- **10 - 20%: International Management and Contemporary Issues:** Value dimensions, regional economic integration, trading alliances, global environment, social responsibilities of business, ethics, systems, environment, government regulation, management theories and theorists, e-business, creativity and innovation.

The exam contains approximately 100 questions to be answered in 90 minutes.

Study Resources:
- Clarkson, *West's Business Law* (South-Western)
- Emerson, *Business Law* (Barron's)
- Miller, *Business Law Today: The Essentials* (West)
- *CLEP Official Study Guide*

Principles of Marketing

The Principles of Marketing exam covers material taught in a one-semester introductory college course. It is concerned with the role of marketing in society and business, consumer and organizational markets, marketing strategy planning, the marketing mix, and marketing institutions. The exam is drawn from the following topics:

- **8 - 13%: Role of Marketing in Society:** Ethics, nonprofit marketing, and international marketing.
- **17 - 24%: Role of Marketing in a Firm:** Marketing concept, strategy, environment, and decision system.
- **22 - 27%: Target Marketing:** Consumer behavior, segmentation, positioning, business-to-business markets.
- **40 - 50%: Marketing Mix:** Product and service management, branding, pricing policies, distribution channels and logistics, integrated marketing communications/promotion, and marketing application in e-commerce.

The exam contains approximately 100 questions to be answered in 90 minutes.

Study Resources:
- Armstrong and Kotler, *Marketing: An Introduction* (Pearson/Prentice Hall)
- Kotler and Armstrong, *Principles of Marketing* (Prentice Hall)
- Pride and Ferrell, *Marketing* (Houghton-Mifflin)
- *CLEP Official Study Guide*

*Remember to buy the paperback edition of your textbook whenever it is available and save $$!

*Source: "CLEP: Exam Descriptions." Copyright © 2011, the College Board. www.collegeboard.com. Reproduced with permission.

Exam Day

What To Bring

On the day of the exam you will need to bring the following to the test center:

- Two forms of identification. The primary one should include your photograph and signature such as a driver's license or passport. The secondary ID should include a photo and/or your signature such as a student Id, social security card, or credit card.
- Any registration forms or print-outs that may be required by the test center. Each test center has its own requirements for registration.
- A credit card or check for the exam fee
- A non-mechanical No. 2 pencil

What Not To Bring

Items that are prohibited by the test center include:

- Calculators
- Cell phones or any wireless communications devices
- Digital watches
- Listening devices such as radios, iPods, media players, or recorders
- Notes or paper of any kind
- Books, dictionaries or reference materials
- Cameras or any kind of photographic or copying device
- Slide rules, protractors, compasses or rulers
- Mechanical pencils or any type of pen or highlighter
- Food and beverages

Be sure to arrive on time. Give yourself leeway and arrive in advance of your exam appointment time. You can not be admitted after the testing session has begun. The test lasts 90 minutes.

Scores

You will receive a copy of your exam score right away when you finish the exam. The only exception to instant scoring is the College Composition exam. Those results are sent within several weeks of scoring. Multiple choice tests are scored by computer. Essays written for the College

Composition exam are graded by college English professors, selected by the College Board. Optional essays for CLEP Composition and Literature exams are graded by the colleges that require them. If you take an optional essay, it will be sent with a copy of your score report (results of the multiple choice test) to the institution you designate on your answer sheet.

Your score shows the total scaled score for each exam you took. Total scaled scores fall between 20 and 80.

If you don't want your scores reported, notify the administrator before you complete the exam. You will be asked to verify that you want your score canceled in the testing software.

Transcripts

At the time you take the exam, you can indicate in the test software, the college employer, or certifying agency that you want to receive your CLEP scores. This service is free of charge only if you select the score recipient at the time you test. A $20 fee will be charged for each transcript ordered at a later date. Transcript request forms can be downloaded from www. collegeboard.com and mailed in with payment to the address on the form.

Joe Takes the CLEP Exam

Joe Wise lives in Buffalo, NY. He is a homechooled student about to begin 11th grade. Joe decides that he would like to start earning college credit by taking a CLEP exam. He reviews a list of exams and descriptions on collegeboard.com and decides on the American Government exam. By preparing for this test, Joe will also fulfill the New York state requirement that a unit of American government be covered in high school.

Joe plans on attending the University of Buffalo after graduating, so he checks the college's website to find out its policy regarding CLEP. The college offers a course that is equivalent to the CLEP exam entitled, "Introduction to American Politics." The course covers the American political system, the three branches of government, federalism, political parties, the electoral process, public policy making, and contemporary political problems. The University of Buffalo grants 3 credits for the American Government CLEP exam with a passing score of 50.

Great! Next, Joe wants to get the study materials that will help him pass the exam. He orders the Official CLEP Study Guide from the College Board website. This will give him sample test questions and answers that he can practice with. Then he checks the list of study resources in search of a college textbook. *American Government and Politics Today: The Essentials,* by Bardes et al. looks like a good one and he finds a used copy for only $17.83 on www.Half.com/textbooks. Another text listed is *Government in America,* by Edwards et al. which he can get from Amazon for $15.99. He checks the Table of Contents in both books and they match the list of topics covered in the CLEP exam. He decides on *American Government and Politics Today: The Essentials,* and orders it.

After the books arrive, Joe wants to find out where the nearest test center is so that he can call and register for the exam. He goes to collegeboard. com and types his zip code into the test center search box. The University of Buffalo comes up. That's convenient! It has a test center right on campus. A phone number is listed with the address and Joe calls the test center to register. He is told there is a registration fee of $25. The center schedules tests on Tuesday, Wednesday, and Friday of every week, from 9 am to 5 pm. Joe schedules his test date for a Friday, four weeks away. He asks if there are any registration forms to fill out and is told that he will fill out the registration information on the day of the exam. On that day he will also pay the test fee of $77 to CLEP. The registration fee of $25 can be paid for in person or over the phone with a credit card and will ensure Joe's place on exam day. Joe pays the registration fee over the phone and his test date is set for the following month.

Over the next four weeks, Joe studies. He reads the textbooks, answers the CLEP practice questions and checks out additional online resources. On exam day, Joe is ready! Before leaving the house he checks to make sure he has two forms of identification, a pencil, and a check for the test fee.

Joe arrives at the testing center at the appointed time and sits down to take the Introduction to American Government test. Ninety minutes later, he is finished. The test administrator scores the test and Joe has passed with flying colors! He can now transter 3 credits to Buffalo University when he enrolls as a student.

www.ingramcontent.com/pod-product-compliance
Lightning Source LLC
Chambersburg PA
CBHW071642050426
42443CB00026B/943